GREAT EXPERIMENTS WITH LIGHT

Phyllis Fiarotta & Noel Fiarotta

SCHOLASTIC INC.

New York Toronto London Auckland Sydney
Mexico City New Delhi Hong Kong

To Frances DiGrazia and Angelina Magliente,
our loving, colorful, and full-of-life aunts, who are
enduring points of light in our lives

ISBN 0-439-16835-X

12 11 10 9 8 7 6 5 4 3 2   0 1 2 3 4 5/0

Printed in the U.S.A.   24

First Scholastic printing, January 2000

CONTENTS

• ○○○○●●○○○ •

WITHOUT LIGHT . . .   5

A BRIEF HISTORY   6

In the Beginning   6
First Uses of Light   7
Lighting Up the Outdoors   8
Lighting the Indoors   9
ABOUT LIGHT FOR YOUR EXPERIMENTS   10

LIGHT TRAVELS IN A
    STRAIGHT LINE   11

Energy Δ *The Speed of Light*   12
Velocity Δ *Nature's Fireworks*   13
Direction Δ *String Highway*   14
Obstruction Δ *Sailor's Friend*   15
Radiation Δ *Light-Ray Fan*   16
Expansion Δ *New Constellations*   17
Size Δ *Shrinking Apple*   18
Transparent, Translucent, Opaque
    Δ *Bright, Dim & No Show*   19
Filtration Δ *Color Tricks*   20
X Rays Δ *I See You!*   21
Heliotropism Δ *Pinched Grass*   22
Communication Δ *Wireless Telephones*
    Δ *Reflected Light* Δ *Direct Light*   23
Darkness Δ *Ant Farm*   24

LIGHT CASTS SHADOWS   25
Close-Distance Projection
    Δ *Mr. Snowman*   26
Far-Distance Projection Δ *Spooky Ghosts*   27
Diffused Reflection Δ *Sharpness*   28
Angle Δ *Save the Fort!*   29
Double Light Beams Δ *Onstage*   30
Indirect Light Δ *Me & My Shadow*   32
Fading Δ *Sun Print*   33
Back Light Δ *Jack-o'-Lantern*   34
Shadow Puppets Δ *My Fair Garden*   35
Shadow on Black Δ *Halo*   36
Silhouette Δ *Sit Still!*   37
Combined Shadows Δ *Animated Tree*   38
Shadow Pictures Δ *Shadow Zoo*   39
Sundial Δ *Making a Sundial*   40

LIGHT REFLECTS OFF SURFACES   41
Scattering Air Δ *Sunbeams*   42
Scattering Water Δ *Aqua Beam*   43
Regular Reflection Δ *Water's Surface*   44
Regular Reflection—Light Beam
    Δ *All in the Angle*   45
Diffused Reflection—Light & Dark
    Δ *Illumination*   46

Diffused Reflection—Texture
  Δ *Helter-Skelter*   47
Diffused Reflection—Color
  Δ *Warm Glow*   48
Heat Δ *Solar Heat*   49
Luminosity Δ *Floating Butterflies*   50
Distraction Δ *Up, Up & Away!*   51
Real Image Δ *Star Target*   52
Virtual Image Δ *Topsy-Turvy*   53
Reversed Virtual Image
  Δ *Time Moves Backward*   54
Multiple Images—Facing Mirrors
  Δ *Fruit Parade*   55
Multiple Images—Connected Mirrors
  Δ *Kaleidoscope*   56
Rerouting Δ *Periscope*   57
Color Blending Δ *Spinning Top*   58

LIGHT REFRACTS   59
Water Refraction Δ *Broken Sipper*   60
Air Temperature Δ *Ghost Flames*   61
Water Refraction—Top Surface
  Δ *Magic Penny*   62
Positive Glass Lens Δ *Microscope*   63
Reversed Image Δ *About Face*   64
Strong & Weak Lenses Δ *Turn Around*   65
Photography Δ *Box Camera*   66
The Eye Δ *Blind Spot* Δ *Pupil & Iris*   67
Vision Δ *The Eye Lens* Δ *Optical Illusions*   68
Concave & Convex Δ *Silly Reflections*   69
Water Lens Δ *Magnifying Water Drops*   70
Cylindrical Lens Δ *Magnifying Bottle*   71
Dispersion Δ *Pumpkin Quartet*   72
Bent Light Beams Δ *Water Beams*   73
Interference Δ *Fractured Reflections*   74
Color Spectrum Δ *Prisms*   75
Double Image Δ *Dancing Beams*   76
Iridescence—Curved Surface
  Δ *Soap Bubbles*   77
Iridescence—Flat Surface Δ *Oil Slick*   78

LIGHT SMARTS   79
In Sunlight Δ In the Dark Δ Eye Savers
  Δ Other Tips   79

INDEX   80

WITHOUT LIGHT . . .

Golden sunflowers would not grow;
Arching rainbows would not bow.

Stars would not twinkle in the sky;
Colors would not reach your eye.

A field of grass would not be green;
A picture book could not be seen.

Fireworks are just booms at night;
Fireflies are just bugs in flight.

But because there is light, a big gray rock
drifting in the vast black universe is bright
with green grass and a blue sky, yellow sun-
rise and orange sunset, violet flowers, and red
apples.

A BRIEF HISTORY

IN THE BEGINNING

Most astronomers believe that the Big Bang, a mighty explosion, created all that exists in the universe. The Earth is over 4 billion years old.

Grass, trees, and flowers grew in the warm sun. In the oceans, simple life forms began to grow. Eventually, fishlike animals crawled out of the water and took their first gulps of air.

The Earth's rich plant life provided food for the dinosaurs. Dinosaurs roamed the Earth for over 130 million years.

Some scientists believe a comet hit the Earth, creating a cloud of dust that blocked the sun's light. Without light, the plants died. Without plants, the dinosaurs died.

FIRST USES OF LIGHT

The first peoples burned fat to cook food about 70,000 years ago. Torches made of dried grasses and fat lit the caves that were their homes.

In ancient civilizations like Rome and Greece, people built houses with openings in the ceilings. Light entered the gloomy rooms through these openings.

Wax candles are 3,000 years old. European monks, during the Renaissance, wrote the earliest books in candlelight.

LIGHTING UP THE OUTDOORS

The moon was the greatest source of light for night-time activities. In many hot climates, people planted seeds during the cool evening hours.

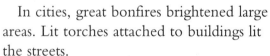

In cities, great bonfires brightened large areas. Lit torches attached to buildings lit the streets.

The earliest flashlights were small clay dishes with burning oil.

LIGHTING THE INDOORS

People began to use oil lamps with glass chimneys and wicks in the early 1700s. Raising and lowering the wick adjusted the flame's brightness as the oil burned.

Natural gas, found deep within the Earth, came into the home through wall lamps. Like burning oil, gas for gaslights caused many accidental fires.

People tried to create a lightbulb that burned for hours. Thomas Edison discovered that a bamboo filament burned longest. The lightbulb, which uses a tungsten (also called wolfram) filament, is considered one of the most important inventions of the 20th century.

BEWARE OF THE GAS

ABOUT LIGHT FOR *YOUR* EXPERIMENTS

Each experiment will vary slightly depending on the natural or artificial light you use. An experiment performed in the dark is brighter and sharper than an experiment in bright light.

SUNLIGHT Sunlight is an excellent light source for many experiments. Some experiments call for bright, indirect light (away from sunlight), like a cloudy day.

INCANDESCENT LIGHT An incandescent bulb has a thin wire (filament) that gets hot and burns when an electric current passes through it. An incandescent lightbulb produces warm light because its light contains more red than blue color.

FLUORESCENT LIGHT A fluorescent tube contains gas under pressure that glows when an electric current flows through it. A fluorescent-light tube produces cool light because its light contains more blue than red color.

BATTERY-POWERED LIGHT A flashlight receives its power from batteries. The size and brightness of a flashlight's beam depend on the size of the lightbulb, the size of the reflective dish, and the strength of the battery.

CANDLELIGHT Only a few experiments call for candlelight. Never use a lit candle without an adult present.

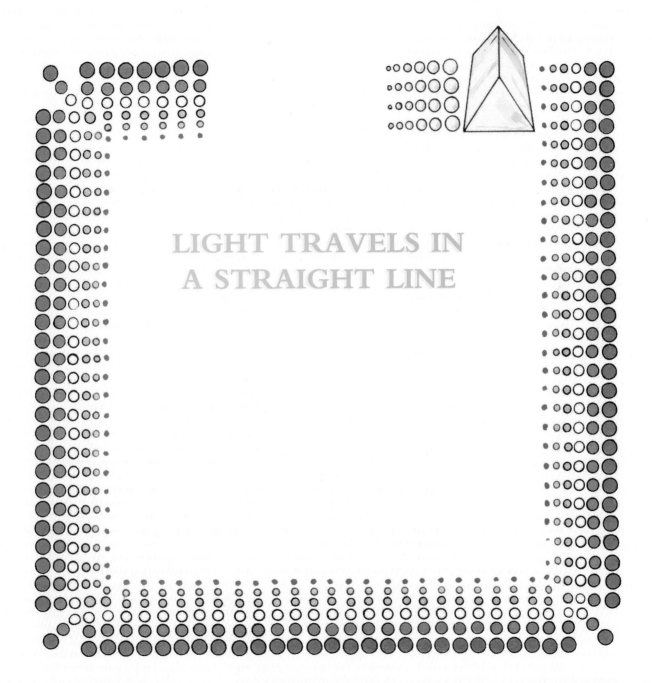

LIGHT TRAVELS IN
A STRAIGHT LINE

ENERGY

Light is energy and energy has the ability to travel. Light travels in a straight line. The sun's light takes 8.5 seconds to reach Earth. The sun, in the center of the solar system, is our most important source of light.

The Speed of Light

CHECKLIST

picture Δ tape Δ ball Δ flashlight

A

1. Draw a picture. Tape it to a wall.
2. In a bright room, throw a ball at the picture (A).
3. Turn off the room's light. With a flashlight facing the picture, turn on the light beam (B).

RESULT

You see the ball travel across the room and hit the picture (A). You do not see the light beam cross the room. It is on the picture the instant the light turns on (B).

B

The speed a ball travels is as fast as someone can throw it. The speed of light is over 186,000 miles (297,600 kilometers) a second, too fast for the eye to see it travel.

VELOCITY

Lightning is a sudden natural electrical flash of light in the sky. In thunderstorms, lightning sometimes strikes the Earth. A metal lightning rod attached to a house or building attracts lightning and grounds it (sends it into the earth).

Nature's Fireworks

CHECKLIST

thunderstorm Δ paper Δ pencil

1. From inside your home, count the seconds between flashes of lighting and claps of thunder.
2. Write down the times.

RESULT

You see lightning before you hear thunder.

Light travels over 186,000 miles (297,600 kilometers) per second; sound travels 1,100 feet (330 meters) per second. As a storm approaches, the seconds between lightning and thunder grow fewer. As the storm moves away, the number of seconds increase. When thunder immediately follows lightning, the storm is directly overhead.

DIRECTION

A spotlight is a strong beam of light that lights up a small area. Spotlights are important in theater productions. Along with stage lighting, a stagehand works the spotlight to follow actors and singers as they move when the stage is dark.

String Highway

CHECKLIST

picture Δ heavy string Δ transparent tape Δ flashlight

1. Tape one end of a length of string to a picture taped on a wall.
2. Tape the other end of the string on a flashlight's lens.
3. Stretch the string tightly.
4. Aim the center of the flashlight's light beam at the end of the string taped on the picture.

RESULT

If you hold the flashlight in line with the string, the light beam travels along the length of the string.

Light travels in a straight line.

OBSTRUCTION

When you look at the leaves of a tree at night, here and there you see small areas of moonlight shining through. In these few places, moonlight is visible because no leaves obstruct straight paths of light.

Sailor's Friend

CHECKLIST

poster board Δ scissors Δ crayons or markers Δ candleholder

1. Cut out a window in the same place on three poster-board rectangles.
2. Draw a lighthouse and water as shown.
3. Fold over the bottom edge of each rectangle and stand. Glasses can help them stand straight.
4. Ask an adult to place a lit candle in a candleholder behind the last window.
5. Look through the windows; then move the center rectangle.

RESULT

The flame that shines through all the windows disappears when one window moves aside.

Light travels in a straight line. It stops traveling when something obstructs (blocks) it.

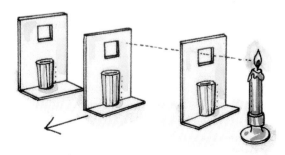

RADIATION

Images on movie film are in frames (boxes) that are a little more than an inch wide, yet they fill up a large theater screen. In 1903 Edwin S. Porter made *The Great Train Robbery,* the first motion-picture Western. In the late 1890s, the Frenchmen Georges Méliès and the brothers Auguste and Louis Jean Lumière made some of the earliest motion pictures.

Light-Ray Fan

CHECKLIST

comb Δ flashlight Δ white paper

1. Stand a comb on white paper.
2. Press the head of a flashlight against the comb with the light beam shining through the teeth.

RESULT

The light beam breaks into individual rays that fan out.

A comb separates a flashlight's light beam into rays and shadows. Only the center ray travels straight ahead. The other rays fan out from the center because light spreads out as it travels outward.

EXPANSION

A constellation is a group of stars that make a picture. Although they move in the sky, constellations never change their shape. The North Star is a bright star in the sky toward which the axis of the Earth points. (When viewed from the Northern Hemisphere, it does not appear to move.) It is the last star in the tail of a Little Bear we call Ursa Minor.

New Constellations

CHECKLIST
foam cup Δ flashlight Δ pencil Δ scissors Δ poster board or cardboard Δ large nail

1. Trace the bottom of a flashlight on the bottom of a cup. Cut out (a).
2. Push the bottom of the flashlight through the hole.
3. Draw a design on a circle cut from poster board (b).
4. With a nail, punch holes along the design (c).
5. With the circle pressed against the lens of a flashlight, aim the light beam at the ceiling.

RESULT
The design appears very large in dots of light. Light beams spread out as they travel. The farther they travel, the more they spread out from each other.

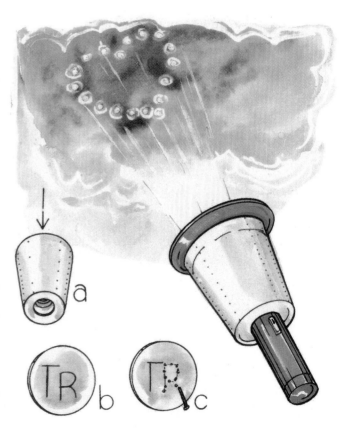

SIZE

Scientists believe the universe is expanding. This means that the planets, stars, solar systems, and galaxies are all moving away from each other. Scientists believe that one day the universe will stop expanding and begin to contract (stars and planets will move closer together).

Shrinking Apple

CHECKLIST

sheet of white paper Δ markers or crayons
Δ flashlight

1. Draw a small apple in the center of a sheet of paper.
2. Tape the paper to a wall.
3. Hold the flashlight close to the paper so that the apple fits inside the light beam. Slowly move the flashlight away from the apple.

RESULT

The light beam on the paper grows larger as the flashlight moves away from it.

   A light beam spreads out as it travels. The farther light travels, the larger the beam grows.

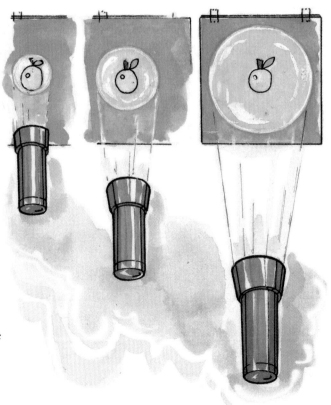

TRANSPARENT, TRANSLUCENT, OPAQUE

Mountains grow lighter in color as we travel away from them and they move into the distance. In our atmosphere (air), there are tiny specks of dust, smoke, and water vapor. The more specks that get in the way, the less traveling light can reach a surface. The less light, the lighter the color.

Bright, Dim & No Show

CHECKLIST
clear plastic wrap Δ wax paper Δ flashlight
Δ construction paper

1. Shine a flashlight beam on a wall.
2. Place plastic wrap in front of the flashlight's light beam (A).
3. Place wax paper in front of the beam (B).
4. Place construction paper in front of the beam (C).

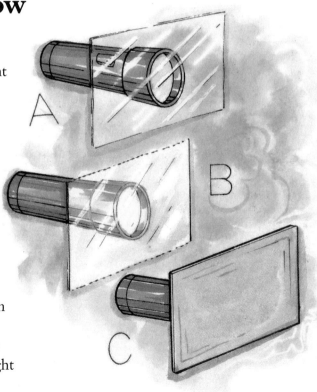

RESULT
Plastic wrap produces a bright light beam, wax paper a dim light beam, and construction paper no light beam.

  Plastic wrap is *transparent*—all light passes through. Wax paper is *translucent*—some light passes through. Construction paper is *opaque*—no light passes through.

FILTRATION

Photographers must develop film in the dark. How can they see what they are doing in the dark? A red light in a photographer's darkroom does not affect film, as does white light, yet it allows the photographer to see what he or she is doing.

Color Tricks

CHECKLIST

colored construction paper Δ scissors Δ glue Δ red and green cellophane or tracing paper colored with markers Δ flashlight

1. Glue white paper lace and a green arrow to a red heart. Glue the heart to a blue background.
2. Shine a flashlight beam on the heart (A).
3. Place red cellophane over the beam (B); then try green cellophane (C).

RESULT

Some colors change in a colored light beam.

Red cellophane allows only red light to pass through. (See Color Spectrum, p. 75.) Red light reflecting off red and white paper reaches your eyes as red. Red light on all other colors is a mixture of red and those colors. Green shining light on green and white paper reaches your eyes as green.

X RAYS

Some squids that live in the deep oceans flash a bright rosy color when they are frightened. Fireflies blink a white light in the dark to find each other. When a squid and a firefly turn on their lights, their solid bodies look transparent.

I See You!

CHECKLIST

white envelope Δ coins Δ fresh egg Δ flashlight

PAPER Press an envelope with coins inside against a flashlight beam (A).

FLESH Press your hand against the flashlight beam (B).

EGGSHELL Hold a raw egg against the beam (C).

RESULT

The coins (A), your bones (B), and the egg yolk (C) are visible.

Paper, flesh, and eggshell are translucent, which means they allow some light to pass through them. Paper is more translucent than an eggshell.

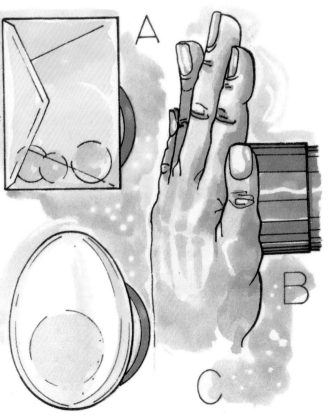

HELIOTROPISM

When a tree falls but does not break away from its roots, it still grows. Although the tree lies on the ground, all its new growth turns up toward the sky. This is called HELIOTROPISM, which is the ability of a plant to grow toward sunlight.

Pinched Grass

CHECKLIST

poster board Δ construction paper Δ scissors Δ glue Δ tape Δ disposable pie tin Δ potting soil Δ grass seed Δ water

1. Roll poster board into a cylinder that will fit over a pie tin. Tape (a). Glue on paper cutouts.
2. Cut out a small hole in the middle of a circle (b) and place it on top of the cylinder (c).
3. In a tin, plant seeds in soil, water, and place the tin in a sunny window.
4. When grass is 2 inches (5 centimeters) tall, place the cylinder over the tin.
5. Remove the cylinder in two days.

RESULT

The tips of the blades of grass bend toward the middle. A light beam can travel through a tiny hole. Plants always bend toward light.

COMMUNICATION

Morse code is a way to communicate with others using short and long flashes of light. The code uses a series of dots and dashes that stand for letters of the alphabet. A short burst of light is a dot. A long flash of light is a dash. (A telegraph uses short and long sounds.)

Wireless Telephones

CHECKLIST
mirror △ flashlight △ friend at a distance

Create a code with a friend using short and long flashes of light. For instance, 4 short and 1 long could mean "Can you come to my house?"

REFLECTED LIGHT
1. Catch the Sun's light rays in a mirror.
2. Make short and long bursts of light by covering the mirror with your hand (A).
DIRECT LIGHT
At night turn a flashlight on and off in long and short light bursts (B).

RESULT
You spoke with light. Interrupting a light beam with an off-and-on pattern creates an unspoken language.

DARKNESS

Some animals live in darkness. Animals like raccoons, bats, and owls sleep during the day and come out at night to eat. Earthworms respond to light by moving away from it. Animals that prefer the darkness are called nocturnal animals.

Ant Farm

CHECKLIST

small can Δ aluminum foil Δ large jar Δ soil Δ water Δ spoon Δ screen Δ strong rubber band Δ water Δ paper bag

1. Cover a can with foil (a). Place it in a jar (b).
2. Fill the jar with soil (c). Add a few teaspoons of water.
3. Add garden ants. Quickly cover the jar with a circle of screen. Secure it with a rubber band.
4. Keep the jar in a dark place for two days before adding bits of bread and vegetables.
5. Now and then, bring the ants into the light to study and feed them.

RESULT

In the jar, tunnels and ants are visible. Ants rely on touch to dig and live inside the dark soil.

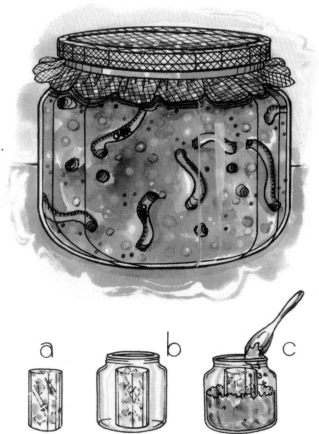

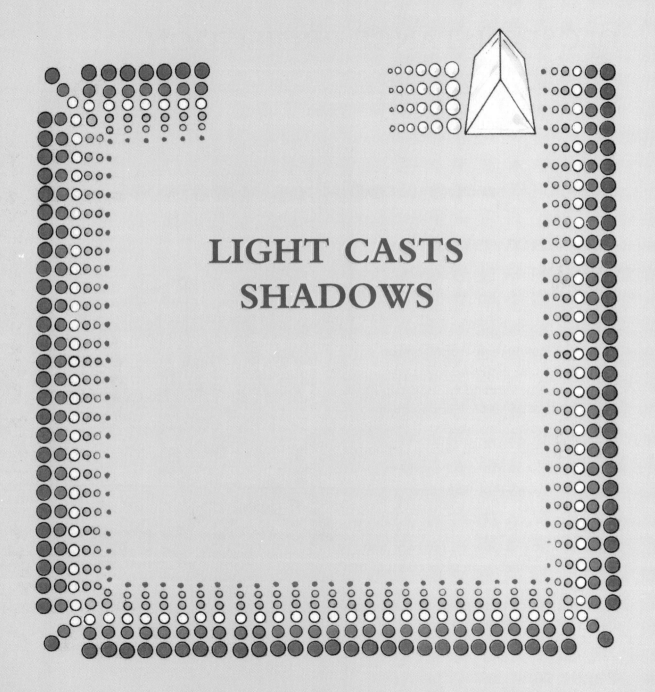

LIGHT CASTS
SHADOWS

CLOSE-DISTANCE PROJECTION

A shadow is the absence of light, which means a shadow is dark, almost black. A shadow on white paper is dark. A shadow on white snow is bluish. Water, whether a snowy landscape or the ocean, appears blue to our eyes when light hits it right.

Mr. Snowman

CHECKLIST

markers or crayons Δ white poster board or construction paper Δ scissors Δ glue Δ flashlight

1. Draw a snowman or a snowwoman with a straight bottom. Cut out.

2. To stand, glue a strip to the snowman's back.

3. Fold a sheet of poster board to create a back wall. Draw snowflakes.

4. Place a flashlight in front of the poster board.

5. Move the snowman back and forth in the flashlight's beam of light.

RESULT

The snowman's shadow on the back wall changes in size. When an object is close to a light source, it blocks most of the light (a). When the object moves away from the light source, it blocks less light, creating a smaller shadow (b).

FAR-DISTANCE PROJECTION

In the sunlight, clouds high in the sky cast giant slow-moving shadows on the landscape below. As the clouds move, their shadows move across the grassy hills and city buildings. Airplanes flying overhead cast large, fast-moving shadows.

Spooky Ghosts

CHECKLIST

poster board Δ pencil Δ long sticks or twigs Δ scissors Δ tape Δ light

1. Draw ghosts, witches, or jack-o'-lanterns on poster board. Cut out.
2. Tape a stick to each cutout.
3. Push the sticks into the ground a distance away from your house.
4. Shine an outdoor light behind the cutouts.

RESULT

The shadows on the house are large but dim.

A light beam loses energy (light) as it travels. The less energy, the dimmer the light on a surface. The dimmer the light, the dimmer the shadow.

DIFFUSED REFLECTION

February 2 is the traditional Groundhog Day in the United States. On that day, people say, a groundhog pops its head out of its burrow (home in the ground). If a groundhog sees its shadow, it returns to its burrow to sleep for six more weeks of winter. If it sees no shadow, spring soon follows.

Sharpness

CHECKLIST

object with a handle, like a spoon or toy Δ flashlight Δ wax paper

1. Hold an object in front of a flashlight's light beam. Study the shadow on a wall.
2. Cover the head of the flashlight with wax paper. Study the shadow.

RESULT

The light beam on the wall is not as strong through wax paper.

Wax paper absorbs (soaks up) some light that passes through it. (See Translucent, p. 19.) The light that does pass through diffuses (spreads out). Diffused light casts shadows less strong than full light does.

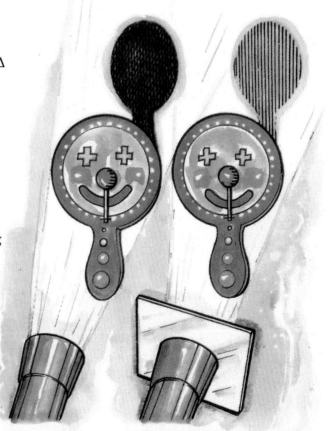

ANGLE

A full moon, a half-moon, a crescent moon, and a new moon (no light at all) are the four phases of the moon. When the Earth moves between the sun and the moon, it blocks light from the sun and casts its shadow on the moon's surface.

Save the Fort!

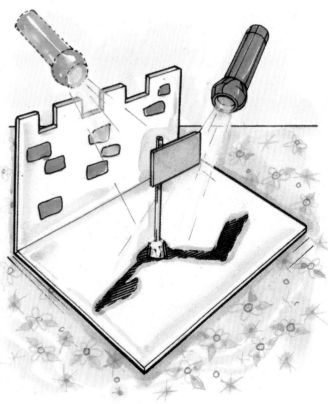

CHECKLIST

sheet of white poster board Δ scissors Δ markers or crayons Δ paper Δ drinking straw Δ play clay Δ flashlight

1. To make a fort, fold poster board to form a back wall. Cut out rectangles along the top of the wall. Draw bricks.

2. Glue a paper flag to the top of a straw. Push the straw into a wad of play clay or a cork.

3. Stand the flag in the center of the poster board. Shine the flashlight on the flag from different angles.

RESULT

The flag's shadow on the back wall appears with different outlines. As you raise a flashlight above an object, the angle of the light beam changes. The steeper the angle, the less light the object blocks, which creates distorted (odd) shadows.

DOUBLE LIGHT BEAMS

White and colored lights above, at the sides, and in front of a theater stage illuminate (light up) actors and scenery from all angles. Light that comes from all directions does not create shadows which would distract an audience.

Onstage

CHECKLIST

2 flashlights Δ white paper Δ food can or plastic cup Δ colored cellophane or tissue paper Δ scissors Δ rubber bands

WHITE LIGHT

1. Place a can near the back edge of a sheet of paper.
2. Hold two flashlights above the can at opposite sides.
3. Turn on one flashlight. Turn on the other flashlight.

RESULT

One light beam casts a long shadow. Two beams cast a triangular shadow. See this page (a and b).

One light beam casts a simple shadow (a). Two beams cross each other and cut away part of the other's shadow (b). This leaves a pie-wedge-shape shadow in between.

COLORED LIGHT

1. Wrap different colors of cellophane around the head of two flashlights. Hold the cellophane in place with rubber bands.
2. Repeat steps 2 and 3 for White Light.

RESULT

The light on the paper at both sides of the can is colored. The triangular shadow is black (A on p. 31).

A shadow is the lack of light; therefore, it doesn't matter what color the light source is (B on p. 31).

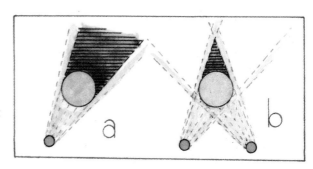

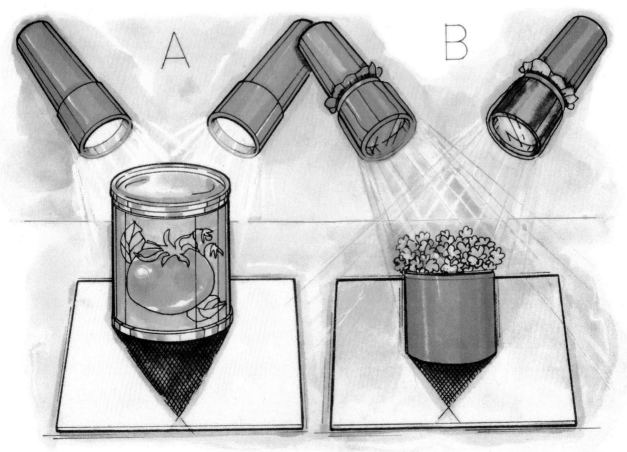

INDIRECT LIGHT

A cloudy day does not create shadows. Photographers prefer to shoot photographs on bright cloudy days because objects and people do not cast shadows that clutter a photograph. Sometimes purposely added shadows make a photograph more interesting.

Me & My Shadow

CHECKLIST

assorted objects Δ white paper Δ bright indirect light

Place objects on white paper in front of a window. The light should be bright without sunlight.

RESULT

The shadows are triangular.

Indirect light is light that does not come directly from a light source. Indirect light that passes through a window diffuses (spreads out in all directions). Light hitting an object from both sides of a window casts a shadow similar to two flashlights that are a distance apart. (Note diagram of ball, lower right.)

FADING

Shady places are cooler than those in direct sunlight. Shade is the shadow produced by a large object, like a house or a tree. It is cooler in the shade because a house or a tree blocks infrared rays, which create heat.

Sun Print

CHECKLIST

colored construction paper Δ scissors Δ
tape Δ sunlight

1. Fold a sheet of paper in half along the length, then along the width (a). Fold over a corner (b).

2. Cut out shapes along the folded sides to make a stencil (c).

3. Open and tape the stencil to a sheet of a dark-colored paper.

4. Place the papers stencil-side up in strong sunlight for a day.

5. Separate the papers.

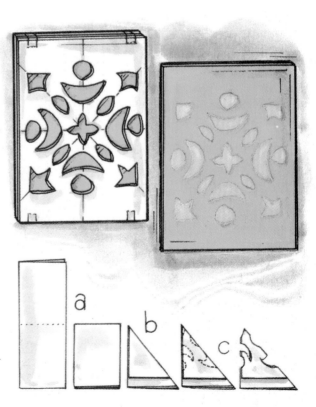

RESULT

The cutout design is visible on the bottom paper. Infrared rays in white light burn away color in construction paper. The color not burned away is the shadow created by the stencil in the sunlight.

BACK LIGHT

In the Northern Hemisphere, the sunny side of a tree faces south. Finding lichen on a tree is a good way to find compass directions. Lichen are plants made up of an alga and a fungus that grow together, often on the shady side of a tree, which faces north.

Jack-o'-Lantern

CHECKLIST
carved pumpkin Δ candle Δ flashlight

1. Add a candle to a carved jack-o'-lantern. Ask an adult for help.
2. Aim a flashlight's beam at the back of the jack-o'-lantern.
3. Turn the lights off.

RESULT
The front of the pumpkin is in shadow, despite the light inside and behind it.

  Light travels in a straight line. Light from behind or from within an object would have to curve and turn around to light up its front surface.

SHADOW PUPPETS

Peter Pan loses his shadow in the room when he meets Wendy Darling and her brothers. Wendy, a very clever girl, sews Peter's shadow to the bottom of his shoes so that he will not lose it again.

My Fair Garden

CHECKLIST

colored paper △ scissors △ drinking straws △ tape △ large white fabric △ broom handle △ safety pins △ cord △ light beam

1. Push pinched ends of straws into other straws to make poles (a).

2. Tape paper actors to the poles (b).

3. Pin fabric to a broom handle. Hang it in a doorway with cord.

4. Aim a light beam at the back of the fabric. Sit on the floor to work the puppets.

RESULT

The puppets appear as shadows on the fabric.

Translucent surfaces like fabric absorb (soak up) some light. Absorbed light illuminates (lights up) the entire surface. A puppet prevents light from reaching the back of the illuminated fabric. This appears as a shadow on the front of the fabric.

SHADOW ON BLACK

The poinsettia is a popular plant during the winter holidays. The red petals are actually the plant's leaves, not its flower. For a poinsettia to grow red leaves, it must be kept in dark shadow for at least six weeks.

Halo

CHECKLIST

black paper Δ object Δ flashlight

1. Stand an object in front of black paper.
2. Shine a flashlight's beam at the object.

RESULT

You can see a black shadow on black paper.

Black paper absorbs (soaks up) most but not all light. The light not absorbed reflects (bounces) out. A shadow on black paper is the color of the paper. Reflected light around the shadow appears lighter black.

SILHOUETTE

A portrait is a likeness of someone. Artists in ancient Greece were the first to cut portraits from paper. In the early 1700s, Etienne de Silhouette of France became famous for his paper-cut portraits. This paper craft was later named after him.

Sit Still!

CHECKLIST
face Δ white and black paper Δ tape Δ light-color crayon Δ scissors Δ lamp Δ paste

1. Tape black paper to a wall.
2. Place a sitter (a teddybear or person) close to the paper.
3. Shine a strong light beam directly in front of the sitter's face.
4. Trace around the shadow with a crayon. Cut it out.
5. Paste the cutout on white paper.

RESULT
You created an exact profile (side view) of a face. An object in a direct light beam (not at an angle) casts a shadow that is an exact likeness of itself.

COMBINED SHADOWS

Although mushrooms grow in soil, they don't produce leaves and flowers as other plants do. Some mushrooms can be eaten, but others are POISONOUS. Never eat a mushroom you did not buy in a store. Mushrooms grow in the dark or in very shady places.

Animated Tree

CHECKLIST
shadow of a very wide tree

1. Stand in the shadow of a wide tree.
2. Extend your arms beyond the tree's shadow. Move your arms.

RESULT
The tree's shadow looks as though it has moving arms.

A tree casts a shadow in sunlight. If a tree is wider than a person, it prevents the person from casting his or her own shadow. When something extends beyond the tree's shadow, like an arm, it creates its own shadow.

SHADOW PICTURES

Meteors struck the Moon long ago and created marks called craters. The Moon's craters and mountains cast shadows in sunlight. The dark markings on the Moon that we see from Earth are the crater's and mountain's shadows.

Shadow Zoo

CHECKLIST

hands △ lamp △ wall

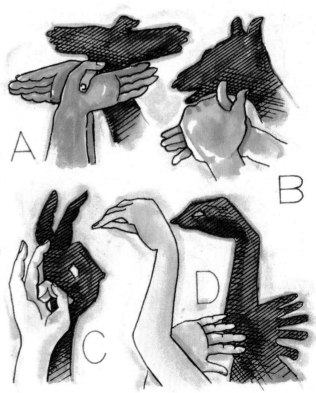

1. Stand close to a wall with a strong light behind you.
2. Arrange your hand or hands to cast shadows on the wall. Experiment with the hand positions shown.

RESULT

The shadows look like pictures. Fingers lose their individuality in a shadow when they are combined with other fingers.

The shadow animals here are a bird (A), dog or wolf (B), rabbit (C), and swan (D).

SUNDIAL

As long as people have watched the sun rise and set, they have found a way of keeping time. The earliest clocks were as simple as studying the shadow cast by a rock on the ground. A water clock uses falling drops of water to tell time.

Making a Sundial

CHECKLIST

poster board Δ pencil Δ ruler Δ compass Δ tape Δ play clay Δ markers or crayons

1. Cut poster-board squares the same size.

2. Cut a square into two triangles (a). Draw a sailboat on one.

3. Using a compass, draw a half-circle island on the uncut square (b).

4. Stand the sailboat on clay balls on the middle of the square (c).

5. Ask an adult to make the slanted side of the triangle face south.

6. Each hour of daylight, note the time and mark where the shadow falls on the island's curve.

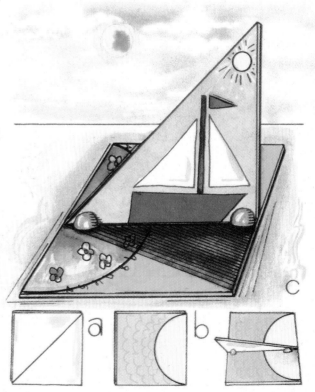

RESULT

Each hour of the day has its own place on the island. The Earth's rotation (spinning) on its axis never changes in speed. Knowing where shadows fall identifies the exact time of day.

LIGHT REFLECTS
OFF SURFACES

SCATTERING AIR

Clouds are water vapor (tiny drops of water) in the high atmosphere. Clouds are visible because sunlight reflects (bounces) off the drops of water. Holes in the clouds allow sunbeams to pass through. Clouds heavy with water look dark because less sunlight passes through them.

Sunbeams

CHECKLIST

cardboard Δ scissors Δ markers or crayons Δ pencil Δ long nail Δ talcum powder or flour Δ washcloth Δ flashlight

1. Draw a cardboard circle larger than the head of a flashlight (a). Cut out.
2. Draw a cloud and sky on the circle.
3. Using a twisting motion, carefully make holes in the cloud with a nail (b). Ask for adult help.
4. Sprinkle a little powder onto a washcloth.
5. In the dark, hold the circle against a flashlight's beam. Shake the washcloth above the flashlight.

RESULT

Light rays are visible. Light reflects off solid particles in the air. When you see a light beam, you are not seeing light itself but light that reflects off particles, such as powder, in the air.

SCATTERING WATER

Light reflects off the surfaces of objects underwater, such as fish-tank bubbles and silvery fish. Some fish live in the deepest part of oceans where no light can reach. These fish are blind because they have no need to see.

Aqua Beam

CHECKLIST

paper Δ scissors Δ paper punch Δ spoon Δ markers or crayons Δ drinking glass Δ water Δ milk Δ flashlight

1. Punch a hole in the middle of a paper square. Add a design with markers.
2. Add drops of milk to a glass of water.
3. Place the square on the glass.
4. In the dark, aim a flashlight beam at the hole.

RESULT

A light beam is visible in the water.

Light passing through water reflects off floating particles, such as milk solids.

REGULAR REFLECTION

Almost all the light that falls on the surface of water, glass, and mirrors reflects off them. This is called regular reflection. In Greek mythology, Narcissus fell in love with his own reflection in a lake, thinking it was someone who lived underwater.

Water's Surface

CHECKLIST

drinking glass △ water △ toothbrush or pencil

1. Fill a glass with water.
2. Hold a toothbrush close to the water's surface.
3. Study the water's surface from above. Study the water's surface from below, looking up through the glass.

RESULT

The toothbrush is visible on the water's surface from above and not from below.

Only the top surface of water reflects the light from an object (a). When you look up through water in a glass, the reflective top surface faces away from your eyes. The light hitting the reflective surface bounces away from your eyes (b).

REGULAR REFLECTION—Light Beam

The Moon does not create its own light. It reflects (bounces off) sunlight. Moonlight shining on the ocean shimmers because ocean water is constantly moving. The rises and dips of small waves create many different surfaces which reflect the reflective light of the moon.

All in the Angle

CHECKLIST

pan or dish Δ water Δ flashlight

1. Place a pan filled with water near a wall.
2. In the dark, shine a flashlight beam at the water's surface at different angles, including straight down.

RESULT

A light beam reflects on the wall at different places, except when aimed directly down on the water's surface.

The angle that a light beam hits a surface and the angle it bounces off it are equal. (Study the diagrams.) The angle of a light beam determines where its reflection hits a wall.

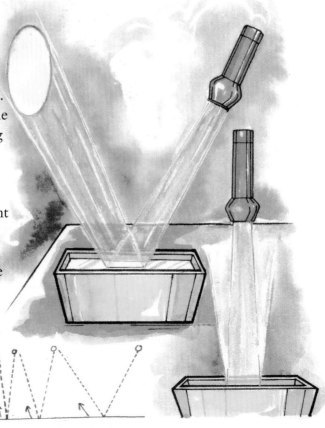

DIFFUSED REFLECTION—Light & Dark

Glass, water, and mirrors reflect most light striking them. All other surfaces reflect some light. This is called diffuse reflection. The moon reflects only part of the sunlight falling on its surface. If it reflected all the sunlight that fell on it, we would not be able to look at it.

Illumination

CHECKLIST

picture △ tape △ black paper △ white paper △ flashlight

1. Tape a picture on a wall.
2. Lay a sheet of black paper and a sheet of white paper in front of the picture.
3. In the dark, shine a flashlight beam at an angle at each paper.

RESULT

The light beam on the picture is brighter when reflected off white paper than off black paper.

Dark colors absorb (soak up) almost all light. Not much light reflects off dark surfaces. Light colors absorb very little light. Most light reflects off light surfaces.

DIFFUSED REFLECTION—Texture

A comet is a rocky chunk of ice that travels in its own orbit around the sun. A comet has a tail made of billions of ice particles that reflect the light of the sun. The tail is not visible as the comet approaches Earth, only when it passes Earth.

Helter-Skelter

CHECKLIST
sandpaper Δ white paper Δ glitter Δ aluminum foil Δ flashlight

1. Sprinkle glitter on a sheet of paper. Place it and sandpaper close to a wall.
2. In the dark, aim a flashlight beam at the papers at an angle, in the direction of the wall.
3. Do the same thing with a sheet of smooth aluminum foil. Crumple the foil, open it, and repeat.

RESULT
The reflections off textured surfaces vary in appearance.

Light reflecting off a shiny surface bounces off it in straight lines (a). Light reflecting off textured (bumpy) surfaces scatters (b).

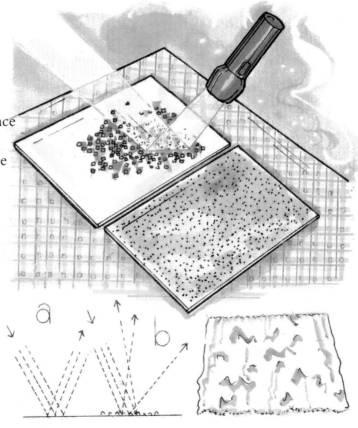

DIFFUSED REFLECTION—Color

As the sun reaches the horizon, its light rays travel directly to you. As the sun sinks below the horizon, the curve of the Earth redirects the rays up toward the sky. The bright colors of sunset occur when sunlight reflects off dust particles in the atmosphere.

Warm Glow

CHECKLIST
flashlight Δ picture Δ red or any bright color of paper

1. Lay a picture on a table.
2. Hold red paper above the picture.
3. In the dark, aim a flashlight beam at the underside of the red paper.

RESULT
A red glow appears on the picture.

Red paper absorbs all colors in a light beam except red. (See Color Spectrum, p. 75.) Blue paper absorbs all colors except blue. Only the color that is not absorbed reflects off colored paper and onto a surface.

HEAT

There are colors we cannot see when light passes through a prism. Ultraviolet rays exist beyond violet in the color spectrum. These rays make skin sunburn. Sunblocks are designed to prevent ultraviolet rays from reaching skin.

Solar Heat

CHECKLIST

2 drinking glasses △ white paper △ sun △ black paper △ tape △ water △ thermometer

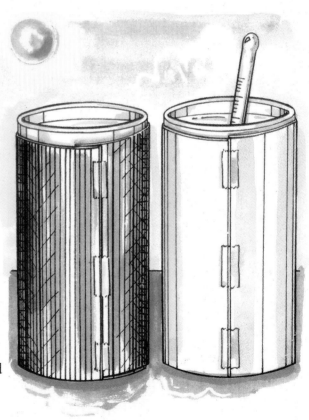

1. Add equal amounts of room-temperature water to two glasses of the same size.
2. Tape white and black paper around the glasses.
3. Place the glasses in the sunshine for several hours.
4. Take the temperature of the waters.

RESULT

The water temperature in the glass covered with black paper is warmer than in the glass covered with white paper.

Infrared rays are beyond red in the color spectrum. (See Color Spectrum, p. 75.) These rays produce heat. White paper reflects infrared rays away from water. Black paper absorbs infrared rays, which heat the water.

LUMINOSITY

Many magician's tricks use the lack of light to trick the eyes. Some tricks use boxes small enough to hold a rabbit and others large enough to hold a person. Because the insides of the boxes are black, an audience cannot see a secret compartment that hides a rabbit or a person.

Floating Butterflies

CHECKLIST

deep box Δ black paper or black paint Δ glue Δ white paper Δ scissors Δ markers or crayons Δ black thread Δ clear tape

1. Cover the inside of a box with black paper (a). Glue in place.
2. Draw colorful butterflies on paper. Cut out. Make a small hole at the top of each.
3. Tie black thread to each hole (b).
4. Tape the ends of the strings inside the box at the top (c).
5. Place the box in dim light.

RESULT

The string seems to disappear, making the butterflies look like they are flying themselves. Black surfaces (string and paper) absorb almost all light. Eyes have difficulty seeing a surface that does not reflect much light.

DISTRACTION

For our eyes to see an object, some light must reflect off that object. When an object reflects light, it is called luminous. The darker an object, the less luminous it is. The moon is the greatest source of luminous light on Earth.

Up, Up & Away!

CHECKLIST

black poster board or fabric Δ white paper Δ markers or crayons Δ black sock

1. Draw a colorful hot-air balloon on paper. Cut out.
2. Tape black poster board on a wall.
3. Put a black sock over your hand.
4. Hold the balloon in your hand with the sock.
5. Move the balloon up and down close to the poster board.

RESULT

You forget the sock and focus on the balloon. A bright surface reflects most light while a dark surface absorbs most light. A bright object is more visible than a black object, because more reflected light reaches the eyes.

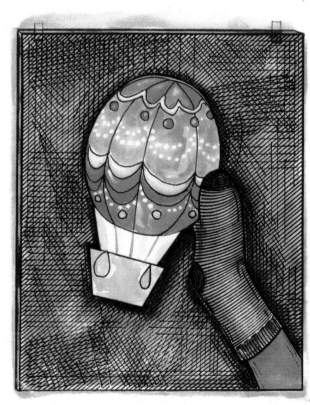

REAL IMAGE

A light beam traveling along a surface is called a real image, which means it is actual light. When a light beam reflects in a mirror, it becomes a virtual image, which means it is no longer real. A virtual image becomes a real image when it travels out of the mirror.

Star Target

CHECKLIST

mirror Δ white paper Δ black paper Δ markers or crayons Δ flashlight

1. Draw a star near a corner of a sheet of white paper.

2. Stand a mirror at the back edge of the paper.

3. Cut a very narrow slit halfway into the middle of a black paper square.

4. Place a flashlight at the corner opposite the star.

5. Hold the square over the head of the flashlight. In the dark, aim the light beam at the mirror at different angles.

RESULT

The light beam eventually hits the star. The angle that a light beam hits a mirror and that it bounces off the mirror are equal. (See Regular Reflection, p. 45.) When you adjust the angle of a light beam at one corner, the beam reflects off a mirror and hits the opposite corner.

VIRTUAL IMAGE

The earliest hand mirrors were found in ancient tombs in Egypt. These were made of polished bronze. Seeing oneself was not the only use for mirrors in the days of old. Armies used mirrors for communication by catching sunlight to send messages.

Topsy-Turvy

CHECKLIST

straight-sided pocket mirror Δ picture
Δ word

1. Stand a mirror at the side of a picture (A). Stand it at the top of the picture (B).
2. Stand a mirror at the top of a word (C). Stand it across the middle of the word (D).

RESULT

Reflections appear backwards (A) or upside down (B, C, and D).

A mirror bends light. A mirror at the side of a picture creates a reversed reflection. A mirror at the top of the picture makes a reversed reflection that appears upside down.

REVERSED VIRTUAL IMAGE

Your face is not exactly the same on each side. Hold a large mirror down the center of your nose. In a second mirror, study your face. The face looking back at you is slightly different than your everyday face.

Time Moves Backward

CHECKLIST

2 mirrors Δ clock

1. Hold a mirror in front of a clock (A). Study the reflection.
2. Stand two mirrors at an angle from each other (B). Face the clock toward one mirror. Study the reflection in the other mirror.

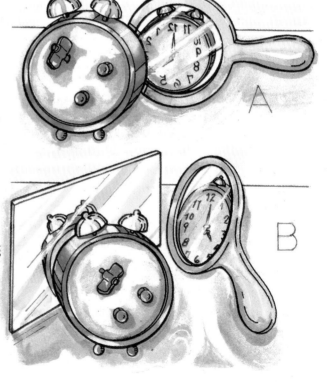

RESULT

The clockface is backward in the first mirror (A). It appears to be normal in the second mirror (B).

A mirror bends light. Bent light rays cross each other and reverse an image. A second mirror reflects the reversed image in the first mirror, returning it to its actual appearance.

MULTIPLE IMAGES—Facing Mirrors

A popular attraction at carnivals and amusement parks is the Fun House. A hall of mirrors is one room you have to find your way through. The mirrors are at angles with one another, which makes it difficult to find the way out. Most times you bump into yourself.

Fruit Parade

CHECKLIST
2 mirrors Δ grape or berry Δ toothpick
Δ cork

1. Push one end of a toothpick into a cork. Push the other end into a grape.
2. Hold two mirrors at a slight angle to each other with the grape standing between them.
3. Adjust the mirrors so that they directly face each other.

RESULT

A curved row of reflected fruit appears in mirrors set at an angle. The row is straight in mirrors directly facing each other.

The reflection of an object between two mirrors continually bounces back and forth. Reflections grow smaller and dimmer as they go into the distance.

MULTIPLE IMAGES—Connected Mirrors

When you hang lights in a window, the lights reflect on the glass. This creates twice as many points of light for the eyes to enjoy. In small rooms, mirrors sometimes cover an entire wall. The reflected room in the mirrors makes the room look twice as large.

Kaleidoscope

CHECKLIST

2 pocket mirrors Δ tape Δ paper Δ markers or crayons

1. Tape two mirrors together (a).
2. Draw colorful shapes on paper with markers (b).
3. Stand the mirrors on the drawing. Experiment by changing the angle of the mirrors or by placing them on different areas of the shapes.

RESULT

The mirrors create a different design each time you move the mirrors.

Light reflects off the shapes and into the mirrors. The reflections continually bounce back and forth from mirror to mirror. As the angle between the mirrors grows smaller, the number of reflections grows bigger.

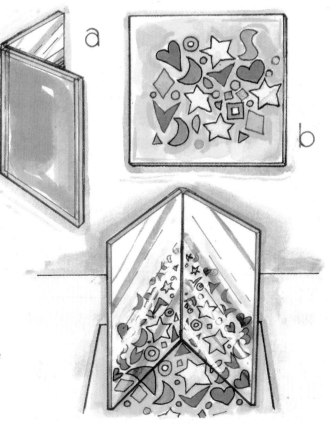

REROUTING

Submarines are made to move under water. There are times when sailors want to see what is happening above the water's surface without being seen. A periscope is a long tube that rises above the water. Mirrors inside allow the sailors to view the ocean.

Periscope

CHECKLIST

long box, like that for spaghetti △ scissors △ tape △ 2 pocket mirrors

1. Cut away a side of a long box. Tape any open ends closed.

2. Cut out a small window on opposite sides of the box, near the ends (a).

3. Tape a mirror inside the box, facing each window at a 45-degree angle (b and c). Ask an adult for help.

4. With one window extending beyond a wall, look into the other window.

RESULT

What is beyond the wall appears in the bottom window.

Objects beyond a wall reflect in the top mirror. This reflection travels to the bottom mirror.

COLOR BLENDING

Red, blue, and yellow are primary (main) colors. Green, purple, and orange are secondary colors. Green is a mixture of blue and yellow. Purple is a mixture of blue and red. Orange is a mixture of red and yellow. All colors are a mixture of the three primary colors.

Spinning Top

CHECKLIST

poster board or cardboard Δ markers or crayons Δ short pencil Δ compass

1. Using a compass, draw a circle on poster board. Cut out.
2. Color the circle in equal sections of red, blue, and yellow (a).
3. Twist a small, sharpened pencil into the middle of the circle (b).
4. Spin the circle on the pencil point.

RESULT

The colors blend into a grayish white.

Light contains colors. (See Color Spectrum, p. 75.) When equal amounts of the primary colors spin, the eyes mix their reflected light into a grayish white. For a **SPINNING GAME**, make a red, blue, and yellow game board (c). The color the top stops on is the winner.

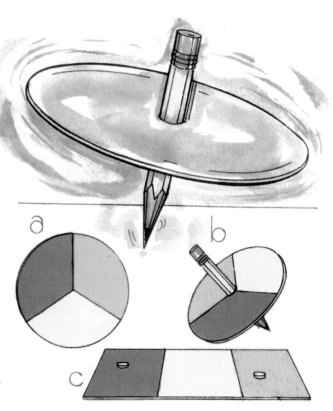

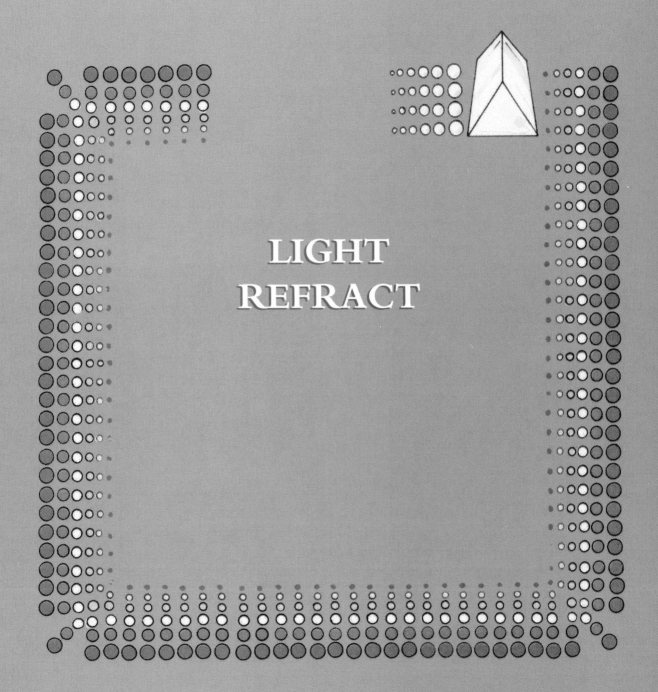

LIGHT

REFRACT

WATER REFRACTION

Light rays change direction when they travel from a liquid into air. This change in direction is called refraction. Refraction happens because light travels more slowly in water than it does in air. That is because water is denser (heavier) than air.

Broken Sipper

CHECKLIST

clear mug or glass Δ drinking straw Δ
clear soda pop or water Δ strawberry or
other fruit

1. Fill a glass with soda pop or water almost to the top.
2. Push a strawberry onto one end of a straw.
3. Put the straw in the soda pop.

RESULT

The straw looks like it is broken in two.

Light reflects off an object in a glass or clear liquid. When the light leaves the liquid into the air, it changes direction. This change makes the object in the liquid appear broken.

AIR TEMPERATURE

When riding in a car on a hot day, you might see in the distance what looks like a pool of water on the highway. In the desert on a hot day, you might see what looks like a lake in the sand. These are illusions, or tricks of the eye, called mirages.

Ghost Flames

CHECKLIST

candle Δ gas stove

With an adult present, study the air above the flame of a candle or the flame of a lit gas burner on a stove.

RESULT

The air above a flame shimmers (glows and seems to move).

Fire heats the air above it. Warm air rises and mixes with cooler air. Cool air is denser (heavier) than warm air. Light refracts (bends) as it travels from warm air into cool air. The shimmering air is light bending.

WATER REFRACTION—Top Surface

Fish appear smaller in a square tank than fish in a globe (round) bowl. If you look straight down into a pond or lake, light can trick your eyes. Fish and other things at the bottom of the pond seem closer to the water's surface than they actually are.

Magic Penny

CHECKLIST

bowl △ coin △ water △ drinking glass

1. Add a little water to a bowl.
2. Place a coin on the bottom of the bowl on a side close to you.
3. Move your head until the coin is hidden by the edge of the bowl.
4. Without moving your head, slowly fill the bowl with water.

RESULT

The coin moves into view.

Light reflecting off the bottom of a bowl of water refracts (bends) when it passes through the water's surface. The height of the water surface determines what part of the bowl's bottom is visible. Study the broken lines (a and b).

POSITIVE GLASS LENS

A positive lens is a piece of glass or plastic that is thicker in the middle than at the edge. Light bends as it passes through the thick part of the lens. The thicker the lens, the more light bends. The more light bends, the bigger the magnified (enlarged) image.

Microscope

CHECKLIST

2 magnifying glasses Δ toilet paper tube Δ picture

1. Study a picture through a magnifying glass.
2. Hold a tube between two magnifying glasses. Look at the picture through the top glass.

RESULT

The image through two magnifying glasses is larger than through one.

A single magnifying glass makes a picture larger. A second glass makes the enlarged picture in the first glass larger. A tube between two magnifying glasses makes an image more clear by blocking out outside light.

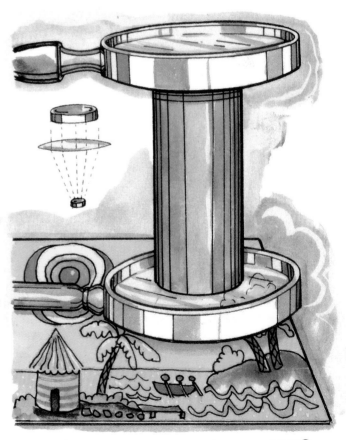

REVERSED IMAGE

Eyeglass lenses are positive lenses. Bifocal eyeglasses have two different strengths of lenses joined. Light refracts when it passes through the line where two lenses join. Refracted light appears in the light's reflection as a dark or a bright line.

About Face

CHECKLIST

eyeglasses Δ photographic slide Δ white paper Δ flashlight

1. Stand eyeglasses on white paper.
2. Place a slide against an eyeglass lens.
3. Shine a flashlight on the slide.

RESULT

The slide's projection (image) is upside down on the paper.

The image made by light passing through film in front of a lens is enlarged (made bigger). If the lens is at right angles with a surface (the paper), the projected image appears upside down. If the lens faces a surface directly—as a projector faces a movie screen—the image appears normal.

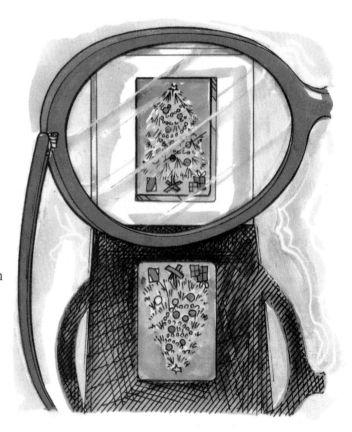

STRONG & WEAK LENSES

A positive lens is either strong or weak. A strong lens is thick in the middle, like a magnifying glass. A weak lens is less thick, more like an eyeglass lens. A giant telescope that searches the sky for galaxies uses one of the strongest lenses made.

Turn Around

CHECKLIST
sunlight   magnifying glass   wall

1. Hold a magnifying glass close to a wall with a window behind you.
2. Move the glass back and forth until the image on the wall is clear.

RESULT
The image of the window is upside down on the wall.

Light rays bend inward as they pass through the thicker part of a magnifying glass. The bent light rays cross each other. The crossing of the rays turns an image upside down. (See Box Camera, p. 66.)

PHOTOGRAPHY

Both a movie camera and projector contain a positive lens. A movie camera captures hundreds of upside-down images on long strips of film. When the film passes the lens of a movie projector, the upside-down images become right side up on a movie screen.

Box Camera

CHECKLIST

half-gallon milk or juice carton   scissors
    wax paper   tape   nail   lamp

1. Cut away the peak of a carton (a).
2. Tape wax paper over the opening (b).
3. Ask an adult to make a hole with a nail in the middle of the carton's bottom (c).
4. Face the hole at a lit lamp or a sunny window.

RESULT

The image on the wax paper is upside down.

Light from the top of a light source enters a box camera's hole and hits the bottom of the wax paper (d). Light from the bottom of the light source hits the top of the wax paper. Light travels in a straight line. It would have to curve after entering the hole to create a right-side-up image. Study dark lines in e.

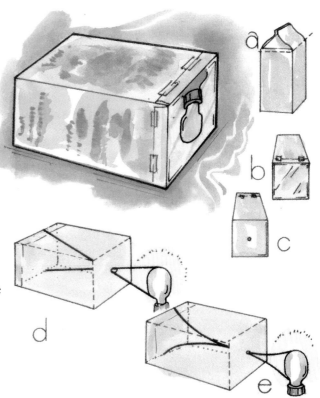

THE EYE

Light first travels through the CORNEA (a), a transparent film. The IRIS (b), a muscle that gives the eye its color, opens and closes an opening called the PUPIL (c). Light continues past the pupil and through the lens (d). The RETINA (e) receives the light.

BLIND SPOT (A)

With your right eye closed, focus on the star on this page. Move your head toward the circle and the star.

RESULT

Slowly the circle disappears.

The eye cannot see light (reflected off the circle) when it hits a BREAK IN THE RETINA (f). Nerves and blood vessels enter the eyeball through this opening.

PUPIL & IRIS (B)

Study the pupil of someone's eye in dim light. Shine a flashlight beam on the eye.

RESULT

The pupil grows smaller when light goes from dim to bright.

In dim light, the iris opens the pupil to allow more light into the eye. In bright light, the iris closes the pupil to allow less light in.

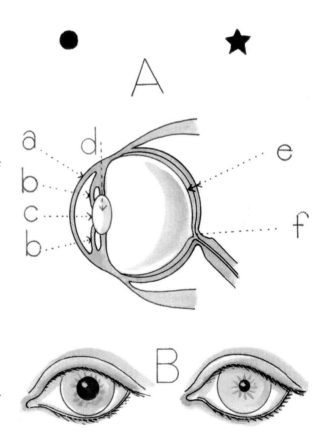

VISION

Most animals and insects have eyes. Fish that live deep in the darkest parts of the ocean are blind because they do not need to see.

Tears lubricate (wet) the eyeballs to keep them from drying out. Blinking helps lubricate them and helps remove pollutants.

THE EYE LENS (A)

The eye lens is a positive lens, which means that it is thicker at its middle than at the edges. When light passes the cornea (a) and the pupil (b), it travels through the eye lens (c), and light rays refract (bend) inward. The bent rays cross each other, turning an image upside down. (See Strong & Weak Lenses, p. 65.)

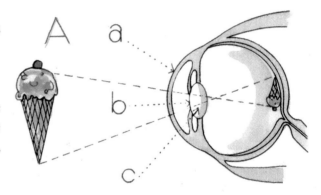

The retina receives the upside-down image. The brain turns the image right side up.

OPTICAL ILLUSIONS (B)

The long lines (d) look curved, but they are really straight. The top line (e) looks longer than the bottom line, but they are both the same size. Such optical illusions trick the mind.

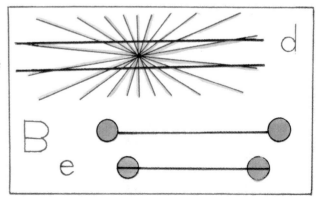

CONCAVE & CONVEX

Not all mirrors are flat. A car's side mirror is slightly convex. A convex mirror bulges out. A car's headlight has a concave mirror. A concave mirror scoops inward like a bowl. A fun-house mirror has a surface that is both concave and convex.

Silly Reflections

CHECKLIST

very shiny metal spoon   Christmas or
other ball ornament

CONCAVE MIRROR

Study a reflection inside the bowl of a spoon (A).

CONVEX MIRROR

Study a reflection on the surface of a Christmas ornament or the underside of a spoon (B).

RESULT

The reflection on the bowl of the spoon is upside down. The reflection on the ornament is right side up.

Light rays reflecting off a concave mirror travel inward and cross each other. See broken lines (a). The crossed rays turn an image upside down. Light rays reflecting off a convex mirror travel outward. See broken lines (b). This creates a normal image.

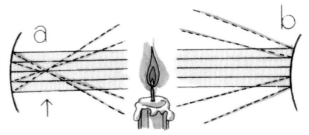

WATER LENS

Why doesn't a large drop of water collapse into a flat puddle? Molecules on the drop's outer surface are attracted to each other (stick together). This attraction creates a rubbery skin called cohesion. Cohesion holds water together, creating a lens.

Magnifying Water Drops

CHECKLIST

poster board   scissors   clear plastic
wrap   tape   printed type or picture
water   spoon

1. Cut out a circle from a poster-board square (a).
2. Tape plastic wrap over the hole (b).
3. Place the square on printed words or on a picture.
4. Spoon large drops of water onto the plastic (c).
5. Slowly lift the square off the paper.

RESULT

As the square rises, the image in each water drop grows larger. A drop of water is a positive magnifying lens, which means it is thicker in the middle than at the edge.

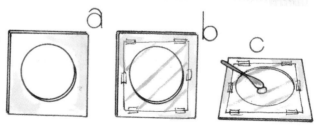

CYLINDRICAL LENS

A snow globe is a glass ball with a scene inside it. The globe contains water and artificial snow that swirls when the globe turns upside down. The scene in a snow globe looks larger than it really is because a glass ball filled with water acts like a magnifying glass.

Magnifying Bottle

CHECKLIST
plastic soda-pop bottle   water
picture or book

1. Remove the label from a plastic soda-pop bottle.
2. Fill the bottle to the top with water. Screw the cap on tightly.
3. Roll the bottle across a picture or a book.

RESULT
The bottle magnifies the image it rests on.

A regular magnifying glass has a positive lens that is slightly thicker at its middle than at its edge. A bottle filled with water becomes a cylindrical (round) lens, which is very thick at its middle. The thicker the lens, the more it magnifies an image.

DISPERSION

Each lighthouse has its own flashing code. After a sailor measures the time between light flashes, he checks a chart to find the location of that lighthouse. A lighthouse's beam is magnified by large lenses so that a ship can see it far away.

Pumpkin Quartet

CHECKLIST

4 glasses or jars, same size   black paper
scissors   glue or paste   food coloring
water   small candle   marshmallow

1. Glue a black-paper jack-o'-lantern face on four glasses.
2. Fill the glasses with water. Add orange (red and yellow) food coloring.
3. Stand a candle in a marshmallow. Ask an adult to light the candle.
4. Arrange the glasses around the candle with their sides touching.

RESULT

The flame lights up the water and appears larger in each glass. A glass of water is a cylindrical lens that magnifies a flame behind it. (See Cylindrical Lens, p. 71.) When glasses touch, light rays travel from glass to glass as well as straight out.

BENT LIGHT BEAMS

Today factories produce perfect window glass. In the past, handmade window glass had imperfections. Things seen through old glass can appear distorted. This happens when light bends as it travels through the glass's concave ripples and convex bubbles.

Water Beams

CHECKLIST

poster board or cardboard   scissors
comb   tape   clean jar or drinking glass
    water   white paper   flashlight

1. Cut an opening on the bottom of a poster-board rectangle. It should be smaller than a comb.
2. Tape the comb over the cutout.
3. Place a jar filled with water in front of a sheet of white paper.
4. Place the comb in front of the jar.
5. In the dark, shine a flashlight through the comb.

RESULT

Some light beams cross each other. A jar of water is a cylindrical lens. (See Cylindrical Lens, p. 71.) Light beams traveling through a lens bend inward and cross each other.

INTERFERENCE

At night on a highway, red reflectors behind cars seem to light up when a car's headlights shine on them. A reflector has hundreds of tiny surfaces that face different directions. The many surfaces reflect light, making a reflector look as bright as a lightbulb.

Fractured Reflections

CHECKLIST

clear marbles, chipped ice, or cellophane
clear glass   white paper   flashlight

1. Place a glass filled with marbles, chipped ice, or crumpled cellophane on white paper.
2. Shine a flashlight behind the glass.
3. Study the reflection on the paper.

RESULT

Marbles, ice, and cellophane sparkle with many points of light and also have reflections on the paper.

Light refracts (bends) when it travels through clear things with many surfaces facing different directions. The refracted light scatters.

COLOR SPECTRUM

A diamond in its natural state is a very ordinary stone. No matter what size, the traditionally cut diamond has fifty-eight facets (sides). The facets face different directions. Each facet refracts light in a special way that makes the diamond sparkle with light and color.

Prisms

CHECKLIST

prism   cut crystal, or faceted-glass object
   white paper   sunlight   cardboard
scissors

1. Stand a prism on white paper in sunlight (A). You can also shine sunlight through a piece of cardboard held in front of the prism with a long, narrow slit cut out of it (B).
2. Stand a cut glass or crystal object in sunlight (C).

RESULT

Rainbows appear on the paper. Light refracts when it travels through two sides of a prism (A), a cardboard slit (B), or through the facets (sides) of cut glass and crystal (C). White light contains colors. Refraction forces light to disperse (spread out) into the separate colors of the spectrum (rainbow).

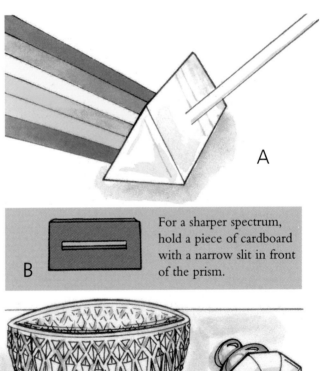

A

For a sharper spectrum, hold a piece of cardboard with a narrow slit in front of the prism.

B

C

DOUBLE IMAGE

A hologram is a three-dimensional photograph on plastic created by a laser beam. When you move a hologram, the image captured inside the plastic changes direction and color. This happens because refracted (bent) light bounces off the many sides of the image.

Dancing Beams

CHECKLIST

white paper   magnifying glass
flashlight

1. Place a magnifying glass on white paper.
2. Shine a flashlight beam on the magnifying glass.

RESULT

Two light beams are visible.

A light beam reflects off the two surfaces of a magnifying lens, the top and the underside. Each produces its own reflection of the beam.

IRIDESCENCE—Curved Surface

A rainbow appears when the sun shines after a rainstorm and the air still contains raindrops. Sunlight, passing through the drops, refracts and separates into the colors of the spectrum. A rainbow is arched (curved) because light travels through curved raindrops.

Soap Bubbles

CHECKLIST

magnifying glass   bubble mix   bubble blower

1. Blow bubbles in the sunshine.
2. Study bubbles through a magnifying glass.

RESULT

Bubbles have many colors.

   A bubble has two curved surfaces a tiny distance apart, the inside and the outside. Light rays passing through both surfaces get in the way of each other. This is called interference. Interference breaks white light into separate colors.

IRIDESCENCE—Flat Surface

A male peacock has beautiful tail feathers with bright-colored "eyes" at the ends. Tiny rods in the feathers lie in such a way that the "eyes" appear iridescent when light falls on them. This occurs because light refracts when it hits the rods.

Oil Slick

CHECKLIST

foam dish   water   black ink
household or motor oil   plastic spoon or disposable dropper

1. Ask an adult for a few dops of household oil.
2. Place a dish in the sunshine.
3. Half-fill the dish with water.
4. Add black ink to the water and stir.
5. Spoon a few drops of oil onto the surface of the water. Discard the spoon or dropper.

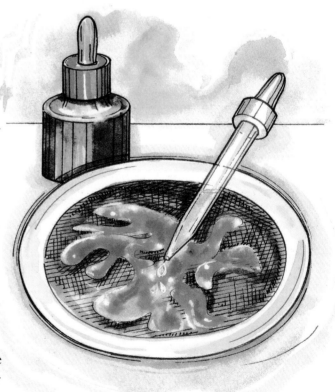

RESULT

Colors are visible on the oil that is spread out on the surface of the water.

Light rays passing through the top and bottom surfaces of a layer of oil cross each other. This is called interference. Interference breaks light into separate colors. Black water helps make the colors visible.

LIGHT SMARTS

Here are some light safety tips that make sense.

IN SUNLIGHT

1. Never look directly at the Sun.
2. Never look directly at a solar eclipse.
3. Do not be fooled by a cloudy, rainy, or cool day. You can still get a sunburn.
4. Use the correct number of sunscreen.
5. Wear light-colored clothes to reflect sunlight.
6. Do not keep colored things that can fade in sunlight.
7. Wear proper sunglasses that block the Sun's UVA and UVB (ultraviolet A and B) light rays.
8. Wear a hat or head covering.

IN THE DARK

1. Walk with a flashlight at night.
2. Add reflective tape to your clothing and bicycle.
3. Always have a light on when going down stairs.
4. Pets, like parakeets, cannot be kept in the dark for long periods. Keep fish tanks well lit.
5. Use a night-light in the house.

EYE SAVERS

1. Always work in a well-lit area.
2. When reading, use the proper lightbulb wattage.
3. Do not sit too close to a television or computer screen, and rest your eyes often.
4. When you have eyestrain, exercise your eye muscles by rolling your eyes around in circles.
5. Never read in candlelight.

OTHER TIPS

1. Read the light requirements for photographic film.
2. Obey traffic lights at street crossings.
3. Obey flashing red lights at railroad crossings.
4. Give flowering plants lots of sunlight. Give low-light plants indirect light.
5. Do not capture lightning bugs.
6. Do not go under a tree in a lightning storm. Stay indoors; close windows.
7. Never ever play with matches.

INDEX

about face, 64
air temperature, 61
angle, 29, 45
ant farm, 24
apple, shrinking, 18
aqua beam, 43
back light, 34
blending color, 58
bent light, 68, 73
bent water beams, 73
bottle, magnifying, 71
broken sipper, 60
camera, box, 66
color
   blending, 58
   diffused reflection, 48
   spectrum, 75
   tricks, 20
colored light, 31
communication, 23
constellations, 17
cylindrical lens, 71
darkness, 24, 79
diffused reflection, 28
   light and dark, 46
   texture, 47
direction, 14
dispersion, 72
distraction, 51
double image, 76
double light beam, 30
expansion, 17
experiments, 10
eye, 67
   blind spot, 67
   as lens, 68
   pupil and iris, 67
eye savers (safety), 79
fading, 33
filtration, 20
fireworks, nature's, 13
floating butterflies, 50
fractured reflections, 74
fruit parade, 55
garden, 35
ghosts, spooky, 27

ghost flames, 61
grass, pinched, 22
halo, 36
heat, solar, 49
heliotropism, 22
helter-skelter, 47
illumination, 46
image
   double, 76
   multiple, 55
   real, 52
   reversed, 64
   reversed virtual, 54
   virtual, 53
indirect light, 32
interference, 74
iridescence, 77, 78
   curved surface, 77
   flat surface, 78
jack-o'-lantern, 34
kaleidoscope, 56
lens
   cylindrical, 71
   eye, 67–68
   magnifying, 71
   positive glass, 63, 66
   strong and weak, 65
   water, 70
light
   bending, 73
   colored, 31
   communication with, 23
   dancing beams, 76
   direct, 23
   double beams, 30–31
   energy, 12
   expansion, 17, 18
   for experiments, 10
   history, 6–9
   indirect, 32
   reflected, 23
   smarts, 79
   speed, 12
   travel, 11–24
   velocity, 13
   white, 30

lightning, 13
light-ray fan, 16
luminosity, 50
magic penny, 62
magnification, 71
microscope, 63
mirrors
   connected, 56
   concave, 69
   convex, 69
   facing, 55
   silly reflections, 69
multiple images, 56
obstruction, 15
oil slick, 78
onstage, 30–31
opaque, 19
optical illusions, 68
periscope, 57
photography, 66
prism, 75
projection
   close-distance, 26
   far-distance, 27
pumpkin quartet, 72
radiation, 16
real image, 52
reflection, 23, 41–58
   diffused, 46, 47, 48
   fractured, 74
   regular, 44, 45
   rerouting, 57
   silly, 68
refraction, 59–78
   water, 60
reversed virtual image, 54
sailor's friend, 15
scattering air, 42
scattering water, 43
shadow(s), 25–40
   on black, 36
   combined, 38
   me and my, 32
   pictures, 39
   puppets, 35
   sharpness, 28

silhouette, 37
zoo, 39
size, 18
snowman, 26
soap bubbles, 77
spectrum, color, 75
speed of light, 12
spinning top, 58
star target, 52
string highway, 14
sunbeams, 42
sundial, 40
sunlight smarts, 79
sun print, 33
surface
   curved, 77
   flat, 62, 78
telephones, wireless, 23
time, backward movement,
   54
topsy-turvy, 53
translucent, 19
transparent, 19
travel
   direction, 14
   energy, 12
   filtration, 20
   heliotropism, 22
   obstruction, 15
   speed, 12
   straight line, 11–24
   velocity, 13
tree, animated, 38
turn around, 65
virtual image, 53, 54
vision, 67, 68
warm glow, 48
water
   beams, 73
   drops, magnifying, 70
   lens, 70
   refraction, 60
   scattering, 43
   surface, 44
wireless telephones, 23
X ray, 21